Breaking Curses
(Pocket Size)

Breaking Curses (Pocket Size)

LEGAL RIGHTS IN THE COURTS OF HEAVEN

Bill Vincent

RWG Publishing

CONTENTS

Copyright © 2020. All rights reserved.

No part of this publication may be reproduced, stored in a retrieval system or transmitted in any way by any means, electronic, mechanical, photocopy, recording or otherwise, without the prior permission of the author except as provided by USA copyright law.

All characters appearing in this work are fictitious. Any resemblance to real persons, living or dead, is purely coincidental.

The opinions expressed by the author are not necessarily those of Publisher.

Book design Copyright © 2020. All rights reserved.

RWG Publishing
PO Box 596
Litchfield, IL 62056
https://rwgpublishing.com/
Published in the United States of America

1

Breaking Curses

Let me just for the sake of explanation briefly explain to everyone about the court of heaven and why Jesus put prayer in three dimensions in the book of Luke. He puts it as approaching God as Father. He puts it as approaching God as a friend, but then he puts it in Luke 18 as approaching God as a judge. I know if you read my other book, "Beginning the Courts of Heaven," but rather than adding to that book, I wanted to expand on this here. And that is the judicial system of heaven where we step before God and deal with legal issues in the spirit that would stop us from getting what God has for us. I mean when Jesus died on the cross, He made provision for anything, and everything we need, **II Peter Chapter 1** says, *"all things that pertain to life and godliness have already been given to us."* So why don't we have it; because sometimes there's something legal in the spirit realm that's resisting us, for instance, when Jesus died on the cross. That was the greatest legal transaction in history.

That's what the cross is. It was a legal transaction. He became sin for us that we might become the righteousness of God. He took sickness that we might be healed. And he actually took poverty so we could be rich, and many other things. And so it was a legal transaction that when we by faith in our hearts come into that with him, we get the benefits of everything he did for us. But the enemy comes through different scenarios to build legal cases against us that do not allow us to get the full benefit of everything. Jesus died for us again. So we have to learn how to approach God not just as our father as important as it is, not just as our friend but also as the judge that is in that place in the spirit realm. We can get everything legally in place so that we get the full benefit of everything Jesus died for us to have.

I was in prayer, and I got my Bible, and it says that the fear of the Lord was upon them all, and many signs and wonders were done through the hands of the Apostles, and the Lord said to me I am upgrading you into apostolic signs and wonders. I'm upgrading you into those dimensions; see I believe we are in a season of an upgrade. I believe that God wants to upgrade you like us into all sorts of dimensions, the new dimensions that God sees, he wants to get us unstuck out of where we have been and move us into the fullness of everything he died for us to have. Now here's the problem. One of the reasons and maybe even the main reason we're stuck, watch this. Is there something legal rights working against us because here's what many people experience, it's like they've got a bungee cord on their back. And it's like they're trying to move forward and all the time they're trying to pull forward, it feels like something's pulling them back. Do you know what I'm talking about? It seems like you're really trying with all sorts of effort to get into the fold as to what God has for you. But something is pulling you back. I want you to know that God wants to cut the bungee cord. He wants to. He wants to break that legal thing that the enemy is using that's trying to keep you out of the fullness of destiny that Jesus has for you. Now let me tell you what that bungee cord is in many situations. It's called curses.

See, one of the things that keep us out of the upgrade that God has for us is or something *that's very real the atmosphere around us, what the Bible calls curses.* And so I want to talk to you about cursing out before I move into them. Here's what I want you to hear. Curses at their core are legal. Curses can only operate against us and our family because they have discovered a legal right to operate. So here's the issue, if you get the legal right of that curse dealt with, then it will be removed, and you'll be able to fully come into everything Jesus died for you now. So here's what I will do. I want to talk to you about what curses are and somewhat how they operate.

So let me just start this. I want to give you keys about curses right here. Number one curses are legal in nature.

In Proverbs 26:2, it says like a fleeting Sparrow, like a flock Flying Swallow. So a curse cannot *be in your life* without a cause. *The word cause it implies something that's legal in other words, it can't just do something because it wants to.* It has to have a cause. It has to have a legal right if you will, to operate against you. I'm talking about some of the things that grant curses legal rights that would be that bungee cord that would be trying to keep us out of the upgrade that God has right to curses. These things have had discovered legal rights to operate against us, and he likens it to birds. That's looking for a place to land.

You see, the Bible says that curses are like those birds that if you let them, if you allow them they will build a stronghold. And if you allow that stronghold to be built, it will pollute and defile everything in you. And when you tear it down, if you are not aggressive, it will come and try to be rebuilt. This is the main thing I'm watching here, that he comes to defile and to pollute issues in our lives and issues even in our family lives. So here's my point. The strongholds are scheming curses that are legal in nature. They cannot land; they cannot operate unless they have a cause. They have found the legal right. Number two curses will only be fully removed in the millennial reign of Christ. Like Jesus, when he hung on the cross became a curse for us.

Galatians 3:13 King James Version (KJV)

¹³ Christ hath redeemed us from the curse of the law, being made a curse for us: for it is written, Cursed is every one that hangeth on a tree:

Therefore there are no curses in the New Testament. Well, here's the problem with that. It says it does, in fact, say that he became a curse for our curses. Everyone that hangs on a tree and that he delivered us from the curse, from the curse of the law but then Revelation 22 verse three says this, and there shall be no more curse. See what's in the millennial reign of Christ. So here's the question when did we become accursed Galatians 3:13a and Revelation 22:3. Because both say, it ended well here. Obviously, the answer is that in Galatians 3:13, that is the stated verdict of the cross that when Jesus died on the cross, he took away the legal right of curses to operate, he rendered a verdict against curses. But if we don't know how to take that verdict and put it into practice, curses will continue to operate against us in our family line. And they will deny us the upgrade that God has, and they will put it in our back that's keeping us out of the destiny of God because every time we're about to step into what we believe we're made for, something knocks us backwards. So, we end up living a life of frustration because we can never quite get into what we actually know we were built for. See, because even though there has been a legal verdict against curses; if we don't know how to appropriate that or execute that in a place, we don't get the benefit of it because we didn't. There will not be a wholesale release from curses until Revelation 22:3 when the full power of the cross is fully in place and there is there. Now across the yard, no more curse they can operate until that time. Here's what we have to do; each person and family has to take what Jesus did and aggressively put it into place to get the benefits of it. So we can walk around all we want, saying there is no curse, there is no curse and being dominated by curses all the time. Being polluted by curses all the time and defiled by curses all the time because we have to know how to step into the courts of heaven and take away the legal right that the enemy is using against us to keep allowing curses to work against us because we will not see the full release of them on a wholesale level until the Millennial reign of Christ.

Up until that time, we have to aggressively put all that Jesus did into place, number three, curses are used by the devil to weaken us. In numbers 22 verse 6, the children of Israel were marching through the land to get to the Promised Land and the king seeing them coming was greatly afraid of them, and so he calls Batum and says, come and curse them for me. Do you remember the story? I mean this is when the donkey talks to him and all this kind of thing and so the bottom line is Balaam ends up going to Balak the king and Balak said to him in Numbers 22:6 therefore, please come at once. Curse the people for me, for they are too mighty for me. Notice he recognizes that God's people are too mighty for him, watch what he said. Perhaps I shall be able to defeat them and drive them out of the land, for I know that he whom you bless is blessed, and he who you curse is cursed, now curse this. So here's what he says to Balaam. Come on, put a curse on them because I need a curse to weaken them so they can be defeated because without a curse working against them, they're too strong. Do you see that? So what the devil use curses for is to weaken us so he can defeat us. This is very important. See, the enemy looks for legal things to use against us as a right. To land curses. If he can find that right, he lands curses against us and our family line so that we are weakened and not able to step into the fullness of everything. Jesus died for us to have the legal right. We can't get into our upgrades. Are you with me? So he uses curses to weaken us so he can defeat us. So he can frustrate us, so we have to know how to deal with the legal issue that is being used by the devil to bring the curse to produce weakness in us because without the curse working against us, we're too strong. That's what even Baylor Greg recognize about the people of God, see what the word of God says, that greater is He that is in us. Than he that is in the world. I mean no. With Jesus living on the inside of us, we are more than conquerors. To Him that loved us.

We are overcomers, but you know sometimes it doesn't seem like we're living an overcoming life. Why? Because there are curses that are operating against us. That is stopping the word of God from manifesting fully in our life. So we have to know how to undo these curses so that we can step out of weakness and enter the strength that God meant for us to walk in so that we can come into the fullness of everything that is rightfully ours. Everything that pertains to life and godliness. Curses are aggressive. They are very aggressive — Deuteronomy 28: 45. Now, I realize in this chapter, which talks about the blessings and the curses, and we understand that because of what Jesus did and because of the new covenant, we're no longer under curses. As far as we understand by faith where we've been seated in position but watch what he says, Deuteronomy 20:45 gives us the characteristics of curses. Watch what he says; moreover, all these curses shall come upon you, watch it and pursue you and overtake you until you are destroyed. He said curses have four stages. They come upon you. They pursue you. They overtake you. They destroy you. That means they're aggressive. See here, here's sometimes the way we approach curses.

Because I did this, my attitude was I get out; I can outlive it. I can outwait it. But let me give you a secret, curses don't end until you stop them. So you can think OK, I can get past this because there was a season of my life when curses came so strong on my life that my attitude was because I'm a "suck it up kind of guy" that I can get things that I can get through this. Anybody know what I'm talking about. I mean I can suck it up, and I can make myself go. I can endure, I can get through this but here is the problem. Before I would even get close to getting through it, something else would hit me. I mean it got to the point that I didn't want to answer the phone or go to the door. Because it was going to be more bad news. I mean it was on one level that was almost comical; it wasn't funny. On the other level, it was like misery because it was just this ongoing trauma and drama after trauma after drama. It is this thing after thing after thing. And I got to the point where I mean it was like the physical thing was not just what was happening. It was that I didn't know how to stop it because I suddenly became aware there was something very strong that was working against me. And I didn't understand the legal nature of the Spirit round with this one. So as I'm walking I'm yelling at the devil or binding; I'm loosing; I'm opening; I'm shutting. I was doing all the stuff I know how to do that I've been told to do, but none of it's working, it's actually getting worse. See, because there was something legal that had been discovered in my life and in my heritage, in my family and in my bloodline that the enemy was using as a legal right to literally come after me with all guns blazing so to speak. And it was it that was allowing curses to land on me and I will tell you they were aggressive. They were coming upon me; they were overtaking me; they were pursuing me once, and they were out to destroy me.

So, in other words, you can't have a passive attitude about dealing with curses. You have to because they are aggressive. You have to become aggressive. You have to become aggressive and say I am going to get things dealt with in my life, and in my history, allowing these things the legal right to operate and you have to declare war against them in the spirit and determined to take the legal rights of them away so that they can be stopped. Because if you don't stop them, they won't stop. They keep on going and keep on going and keep on going. And so the problem for me was I didn't know how to stop them. Because I know I was doing all the spiritual stuff I had been told to do, but I didn't understand the legal nature, and so thank God, there is mercy. He began to unveil that. And as he began to show me the legal nature of the sphere around then, I was able to deal with the source of the situation, and the moment that I did, all the stuff stopped. It all stopped, and I was able to come into liberty and into freedom. But curses are aggressive.

Number five, curses result from iniquity in the bloodline. Now they can result because I've seen or committed transgression and not dealt with it, but I find that most of the time.

The majority of the time, curses are issues connected to iniquity. That's in the blood. That is it, the sin of your forefathers. That the enemy is using as a legal right to operate against you, I probably said this last time I was here but see a really good picture of this in second Samuel 21 when there is a famine in the land of Israel for three years. And after three years, David finally asked God Why. Because they've been praying that they do what we do well, we just need to pray more. The reason this is happening is that we have not prayed and listened enough yet, that is a very wrong perspective. I personally believe that I always know because it just got to the place that worries me that I'm just told I haven't done something enough. We'll see. See watch. We usually need to do something, but it's not that we haven't done something enough, it is that we have not done the right thing. *David and they have been praying for three years to deal with the famine that's in the land.* Nothing changing. It's only getting worse. So David after the third year, says to God, Why? And God says glad you finally ask. Here's the reason Saul, your predecessor 70 years ago, broke covenant with *the Knights* because Joshua swore to protect them. He broke the covenant with them, killed some of them, and because of that broken covenant, there is now a famine in Israel, and this famine will not end until you deal with that broken covenant.

So David goes to give an answer says hey guys, what have I got to do to fix this. And they can give him their demands. David does it. And the Bible says there is God. He did the prayer for the land. See, In other words, the famine ended because God was now free to answer their prayer because the legal thing that was allowing the curse of famine to operate against them was now dealt with because of the broken covenant. It was removed out of the way so that the breakthrough of God could come when God's people ask him. Are you getting this? Sometimes it sounds spiritual, but sometimes more prayer is not the answer. That sounds fairly spiritual. But see, sometimes the answer is, Lord, what is the legal right? *The enemy is using his rights here to let this curse operate against us. And if I can discern that and understand it, I can deal with it. And then God will heed my prayers.*

See, I need you to understand that some of us may need to repent for places, we broke our word for things we have sworn and have not done because they can be legal issues the enemy uses to withstand us. Does that make sense to you? *So, broken covenants, broken words can be big things that the devil uses, so things happened but listen David had not even done this. This had been in the lineage. This was the end. The history of the bloodline of Israel, and because of that, the enemy had taken that as a legal right. Seventy years later to bring this, so sometimes we need to repent not just for what we have done but also for what our ancestors might have done. And say, Lord, we are repenting from any placed curse. There has been a broken covenant that would allow famine on any level to come into our life and or to come into our situation.*

Another thing curses do is they delay and deny. Destiny's curses can delay and deny destiny. In other words, remember we're talking about being upgraded into what we're made for. I mean that was the word this morning—— we're being upgraded. God wants to upgrade us. Well, sometimes, the thing stopping our upgrade is that there's a curse working against us. Isaiah 43:26-28 says it. Here's what he said. Put me in remembrance. That means tell me what I wrote in my book; also the word of God says each one of us has a book, have a prophetic understanding of what you're made for.

That means God and us contending against any legal case the enemy has against us. State your case. See, we're in court. State your case that you may be acquitted. And then he says your first Father's sins. That's bloodline, and your mediators have transgressed against me. That mediators were those that had the right to stand in the courts which are all of us now as kings and priests to our God. The mediators have transgressed; in other words, they had lost their right, and just as a point of reference Zacharia three is a picture of this war that Joshua the high priest has on unclean garments. He is, therefore, as the priest disqualified from presenting cases in the court. And so the angels and the prophets have to give him good clean garments so he can stand before the Lord and begin to present cases again. Now we stand before the Lord based on his righteousness but there are times when we just need the blood of Jesus to cleanse us so that we can stand without shame, without condemnation, without guilt before the Lord and say, Lord, we're bringing this case to you, so it's saying that one of the reasons as I finish this scripture that this is happening is because your mediators those who have a right to present cases have transgressed, they haven't dealt with their own sin. So, as a result of all of that, therefore, I will profane the prince of the sanctuary. I will give Jacob to the curse and Israel to the reproach. So, in other words, he said there's a curse against you as a nation that's operating against you. That is denying you a destiny that God has for you as a nation because a curse is working on you and working against you. So we have to remove these curses to get into the destiny God has for us again. That's that bungee cord on our back. And so we have to learn how to step into this place.

The reason I am so passionate about this is that this revelation about how to move into the legal realms of the spirit into the courts of heaven is because it is what he's done in my life. I battled so much in my life and ministry. I nearly gave it all up. I lost my friends, supporters and even those that I never thought would abandon me because for years and years and years and years decades, in fact, I had people promise me things only to see them break their word. That's just what would happen. They would break their word, and I would never see what they actually promised me that they wouldn't. I became very frustrated. In fact, I may have become a cynic because I got to the point I didn't believe anything anybody else told me because they would promise me all sorts of things only for the words to be broken and my wife would say to me why does this always happen. I don't know why this is happening. And so we would just go through this, and so I came to a place where you know my ability to dream. I kind of lost it. It's like okay. This is what I'm called to do. This is what I'm if this is the realm of influence I'm supposed to have. That's fine; I'll do it. That's good for me. Oh, I'm trying to be something I'm not supposed to be because everything I was pushing for, I thought it was from the Lord. But if that's not what I'm supposed to do, then that's fine. Well, in the midst of my frustration, in the midst of just broken promise after broken promise, after broken promise that people made to me, I had a dream and in my dream there was a present-day judgment against me from a court a legal system in my dream, there's like in it a very real natural way.

Therefore the devil has had the legal right to steal your dreams away. In other words, my destiny that upgraded that we're talking about and so I got up, and I went to prayer, and I repented before the Lord for any place I had walked in negligence. The curse was all the broken promises working against me. It was like this repetitive pattern, so you can usually tell a curse because it's the pattern that just keeps repeating itself, repeating itself, repeating itself. By the time you're going to come into a new realm, here's this thing, it happens again and then you say okay this time, and then it happens, and then you get like this time and then this is destroyed again. See, that's a repetitive pattern working against you and is usually associated with a curse. So, we have to know how to deal with our own stuff but go before the courts of Heaven, before God the judge and say Lord we're asking and we're repenting not only for my sins but for the sin of my bloodline. Remember, this is what Nehemiah, Daniel, all of them did in seeking to get Israel out of the Babylonian Captivity and into the Promised Land. Remember, they repented of their sins and the iniquity of their forefathers because it was the iniquity of the forefathers that had allowed the enemy the legal right to take them captive in the first place. So if we're going to come out of bondage, if we're going to come out of a place where we can never quite get into what we were built for, we're going to come into the upgrade if we're going to get the things broke off our back. Then sometimes we have to say Lord any legal thing personally or in my bloodline that the enemy is using, I'm asking for it to be removed so that curses that are denying me my destiny can be broke and can be removed.

I believe that these keys will help you break every curse and see the blessings of the Lord release the anointing suddenly.

About the Author

Bill Vincent is no stranger to understanding the power of God. Not only has he spent over twenty years as a Minister with a strong prophetic anointing, but he is now also an Apostle and Author with Revival Waves of Glory Ministries.

Bill offers a wide range of writings and teachings from deliverance, to experiencing the presence of God and developing Apostolic cutting edge Church structure, drawing on the power of the Holy Spirit through years of experience in Revival and Spiritual Sensitivity. Bill now focuses mainly on pursuing the Presence of God and maintaining Revival.

His books 50 and counting has since helped many people to overcome the spirits and curses of Satan.

Recommended Books

Recommended Books
By Bill Vincent
Overcoming Obstacles
Glory: Pursuing God's Presence
Defeating the Demonic Realm
Increasing Your Prophetic Gift
Increase Your Anointing
Keys to Receiving Your Miracle
The Supernatural Realm
Waves of Revival
Increase of Revelation and Restoration
The Resurrection Power of God
Discerning Your Call of God
Apostolic Breakthrough
Glory: Increasing God's Presence
Love is Waiting – Don't Let Love Pass You
By
The Healing Power of God
Glory: Expanding God's Presence
Receiving Personal Prophecy

Signs and Wonders
Signs and Wonders Revelations
Children Stories
The Rapture
The Secret Place of God's Power
Building a Prototype Church
Breakthrough of Spiritual Strongholds
Glory: Revival Presence of God
Overcoming the Power of Lust
Glory: Kingdom Presence of God
Transitioning to the Prototype Church
The Stronghold of Jezebel
Healing After Divorce
A Closer Relationship With God
Cover Up and Save Yourself
Desperate for God's Presence
The War for Spiritual Battles
Spiritual Leadership
Global Warning
Millions of Churches
Destroying the Jezebel Spirit
Awakening of Miracles
Deception and Consequences Revealed
Are You a Follower of Christ
Don't Let the Enemy Steal from You!
A Godly Shaking

The Unsearchable Riches of Christ
Heaven's Court System
Satan's Open Doors
Armed for Battle
The Wrestler
Spiritual Warfare: Complete Collection
Growing In the Prophetic
Faith
The Angry Fighter's Story
Understanding Heaven's Court System
Restoration of the Soul
Spiritual Warfare Made Simple
Aligning With God's Promises
Deep Hunger
Beginning the Courts of Heaven

Web Site:
www.revivalwavesofgloryministries.com

www.ingramcontent.com/pod-product-compliance
Lightning Source LLC
La Vergne TN
LVHW092037190726
843493LV00002B/719